Men-Hat

The Poet

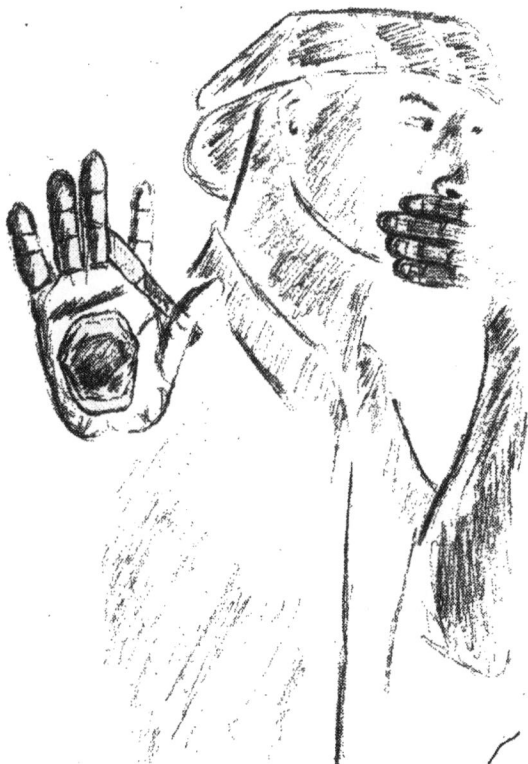

The Strength of Words

Silent Screams

—————— *Silent Screams* ——————

A Collection of Poems

Featuring original drawings by Poet and Artist

Men-Tal

Published by G Publishing, LLC

Editor: Francene Ambrose-Gunn

ISBN: 0-9788536-7-9

Library of Congress Control Number: 2006909231

Published and printed in the United States of America

www.gpublishingsuccess.com

The Ballad for an Angel
was written
in loving memory
of a beloved
friend and brother
Mr. Larry Ricks

ACKNOWLEDGMENTS

First I would like to thank the Most High God for blessing me with the gift of life, love, family, friends, the gift of spoken word, and a voice to share it. I thank God for blessing me with two precious jewels my daughter Tierra Christian, and my son Melvin Christian the third. I thank God for giving me a mind to see the hidden secrets of a cruel world, and the wilds that await us.

I'd like to thank my mother for raising me to the best of her ability. For placing a roof over the heads of our family, clothes on our backs, and food on our table. I know that life was a struggle for her, but she made a way, and I love her for that.

Next I would like to thank my father who taught me the one thing I needed more than anything, and that was to stay focused upon the spiritual side of life, something I treasure deeply. I thank God for blessing me with six beautiful siblings Marcus Lusk, Marketta Lusk, Marletta Lusk, Andre Jones, Brian Christian, and my baby sister Jesica Christian. Special thanks to Dolorous Christian, and Larry Carter for all the literary support. I'd like to thank my brother by Honor, and loyalty Edward Watkins aka Yogi G for being there for me all my life, and being the spark that got me on my lyrical mission, I love you. I want to thank my poetic teachers Abiodun Oyewole, Umar Bin

Hassin, and Babatunday better known as the Legendary Last Poets. Very special thanks to my family, and friends who supported me in my quest to achieve my goal Dana Lusk aka Fattz, Marcus Lusk, Jr.; Aunt Georgia, Aunt Cheryl, Aunt Rhonda, Laquanda, Uncle Peg, and all the children of the Lusk family, Nathan, Darnell, and the Talley family, Maurice Ingram, Joan Ingram, Lamar Ingram, Sherard Ingram, Aunt Myrtle Ingram, Mike Nixon, Derek Rogers, Randy Tumpkin, Aunt Diane Tumpkin, Stacy Tumpkin, Nichole Thompson, Simon Andrews, Nateisha Lee, Dee Lee, Khia Shaw, Rosalind Reed, Mamma Reed, Tracy, Carlos, T.Y, T.J, Curt, Mia, Mya, Marvalisa Coley an artistic genius, Larry Ricks, Greg McKenzie, Booker T. Davis, J-Dog, Micah Adams, J.R aka BLK a lyrical master, Scurve, Danny, Chuck and the A-Block, Chappy, J-Mo, my brothers for life Ira Dixon aka Skee, Vincent R. Towns, Michael Adams aka Diesel and there families, Young Juan Garrett, Shemika aka Miko, Dave Cantrell, Creepy Deezee, Renzo, Showtime, Joe aka Snake, Mike Status, Big tone, Big Moe, Fat Moe, Pam, Scriptures, Vivian Mason, Wood, Diane Moore aka The Grand Diva and family, Big Rob, Los Alini, Damon aka Cutty Fam, Darlene Cleveland, Moe Nitty, Walt, Big D, Uncle Ken, Merrick, Karl G, Gary, Chris Cooper, and the rest of my WTAP fam, Charlett Braxton, the Filthy Paw family, and anyone whom I didn't mention. I love you.

I'd like to give special thanks to my entire poetry family such as The Last Poets, Pharoh who introduced me to the poetry world, Paradise, Carlton, and all of Bout Time, my *sista Zion who took me under her wing, Meeka, Sparrow, Batiyah, Blk, Kim Arie, Knowledge Born Truth Allah, Gemini, PMP, Ameere, SoulSpeak, Ben Jones, Versus, Phoenix, Cassie, Black Ink collective, Omari, Righteous, Reonna, Hardcore, Nicky of Third Eye Open, Raku, Millian, Mamma Acid, Shawna, Mary, Marsha Carter, Marcus, Solomon, Butter, Angel A, John, Ebrohiem, and all of Straight Time, Black Solomon, Ebonics, Andrea, Nichole Wells, Nightwritter, of The Divas of The D, Khan, Symonia of Khaos, Fluent, Legacy, Black Barbie, Wednesday, The Detroit Poet, Rappin for Change, Paige, Dink, Que, and all of the 546 collective, self, J-Nonstop, Sin, Sincere, Volcano, Skiz, Monica Jones, Taneshiwa, Cheryl, Potential, Kalima, Tom, Berhenda, Balou, Londel, Karega, Future, Ayo, and all of flint town poetry collective, Kaniky, Frank the Q, Tenacious, D-Flo, Reukiya Shabazz, Malik El Shabazz, Rhapsody, Bruce George, Big Bob, Marchelle, My Idle Family Gloria Fikes, Mr.Meeks, all the cooks that make sure we eat good everyday at the poetry in the woods festival, my brother for life Anthony "The Boogieman" Rucker, and Mrs. Rucker, Reggie Gibson, Kola Rum, Goldie, Black Ice, Ameere. Thank you all for the impact that you have had in my life with your words, and the friendships that grew from it. Special thanks to Abiodun Oyewole for taking the time to show me the importance of expanding my range of thought, my vocabulary, and how to give my lyrics color.*

DEDICATION

These words are dedicated
To the masses that long
For there cries to be heard
But have not the voice to speak

To that person
Seeking peace of mind
Through soothing words

To all of those
In the depth of struggle
And feel alone
For you are not

To those of you
Who posses the gift
Of art and craft
Never burry your talent

Also to Michelle Stanton
For revitalizing
A very important part of my life
Showing me I could love someone again

And last but not least
To my dear sista Kim Bates
For motivating me
To believe again

Silent Screams

CONTENTS

Acknowledgments   6
Dedication   9

JUST A THOUGHT

Between God and sin   16
Dreamer   17
A trip to Boston   18
Chardonnay moon   20
Sunday dinner   21
Credit   23
Beyond our means   24
A soldiers last words   25
No toilet paper   27
Lazybones   28
Ballad of a bald man   30
Homeless in January   31
Endangered species   32
Old folk young folk   33
If I were blind   35
War and glory   36
Cords of electric   38
One year down and twenty-nine to go   39
A cry for unity   41

Devine inspiration (inspired by Oprah W.)   42
Ballad for my mother   44
Responsibilities   47
Fat Man   48
Lean on Me   49
Idlewild   52

LUST AND DESIRE

Taboo   54
Sexy sista   59
Coffee Brown   60
Chocolate in an hourglass   62
A sista's portrait   66
A sista and her hair   68
Fingertips and toes   70

PASSION AND LOVE

Adore   76
Enchanting   77
Hot tub   78
Climax   80
Her lips   82
The strength of pussy   84
Spend My Life With You   87
Love's worth   88
Soul mate   89
One   91

WHEN RELATIONSHIPS CRUMBLE

Overzealous   94
Issues   95
Picture   97
When relationships crumble   100
Can't let it go   101
Gone   102
Apology   103
Before we sleep   105
Why   106
Separate ways   107

ONCE IT'S OVER

No more us   110
Trap   111
Baby mamma drama   112
Mo drama   114
Young mother   116
A hoe   117
Michigan Ave.   118
Ballad of a fatherless child   120

SILENT SCREAMS

Diary of a slave   125
Brotha man   130
Captive   132

Vigilante   134
Appetite for war   135
Death or a cell block   137
Gangsta'z fate   142
Numbered steps   143
Death   144
Spilled liquor   146
Ballad for an angel   147
Cease fire   148

THE REVOLUTION

What happens   152
The vision   155
Literary leaders (inspired by the Last Poets)   157
Black Unity   160
If my words had no purpose   162

About the Author   165

PART ONE

Silent Screams

JUST A THOUGHT

BETWEEN GOD AND SIN

Between God and sin
You will find me
Torn passionately
Within the two

Why is it that
I love things
That are detrimental to soul
And ignore
The things
That I must do

Why is it
That the ways of sin
Taste so sweet
Yet
Its outcome can be
So blight

Truth is
I wager my soul
For moments of pleasure
With hopes to
Bury my sins
Before my day of judgment
That I may have my soul right

When I face God

DREAMER

You can fantasize
All you want
About prosperity
Your plots
Your plans
And schemes

But
Unless one puts forth
The effort
To place their
Ideas in motion…

Nothing
Will ever come to a sleeper
But dreams

A TRIP TO BOSTON

I took a trip to Boston
On the Greyhound bus
While staring out the window
Pondering life
As time passed me by

On my journey
To the town of beans
I watch as city streets
Blend into dirt roads
And the ever changing complexion
Of a placid sky

I witnessed
Multiple shaped and colored faces
From all walks of life
And intriguing places
While embracing a moment
I never wanted to end

Meeting new friends
That I would never see again
Unless it was destined
That we'll look face to face
And shake hands
On our trip
Back to Michigan

CHARDONAY MOON

Dear moon of Chardonnay
With fatigue print
Upon your face

Your existence
Is so mysterious
Oh bright eye of outer space

You speak to me
With your glare
Though I
Know not what it is you say

But it's your whispers
That guide me through darkness
Oh precious moon
Of Chardonnay

SUNDAY DINNER

There's nothing
Like leaving church
And trying to find a parking spot
In front of Big Mamma's house
Or the neighbors house
Next door

As soon
As you set foot
On the front porch
You can taste the aroma
Of collard greens
Baked chicken
Macaroni and cheese
Before you step on
The living room floor

Auntie in the dining room
Yelling six no!
Uptown!
Grand kids running around
Old school melodies
Sound so reminiscent and sweet

Enter the kitchen
And give Big Mamma a fat kiss
On the cheek
I'm rest ta eat

And ain't no reason for me praying
Cause this batch of food she jus cooked
I already said grace for it last week

I'm ready to get collard green high
From Big Momma's pot liquor
And enjoy dinner with family and friends
From next door

And sad to say
Those precious days of old
That kept us whole
We jus don't seem to wanna live them no mo

CREDIT

From jump
My credit was considered poor
Therefore I started off
In the hole

Who am I
But the average
Everyday brotha trying to
Make a living
And turn pennies
Into gold

If only I would've known
That this system was designed
To keep the rich man rich
And the poor man
Struggling from check to check

I would never have
Carried the burden
Of poverty and stress
Nor allowed myself
To be submerged in debt

BEYOND OUR MEANS

Having
Lots-a
Clothes
Jewels
Cars
And a fat crib
Is nice and all

But what's the use
If you're penny pinching
Just to maintain

Trying to live like the joneses
And laugh
With the big wigs
Till financial crisis
Overwhelms

Then all that
Hard work
And lofty living
Will be in vein

A SOLDIER'S LAST WORDS

This battle field is cursed…

My last breath awaits me…

At this moment
There's no such thing as home
Family nor friends
The heart must be frostbitten
If you wish to have any chance to survive

On these misty war grounds
Life is surreal
Food may come from my next kill
Just to fill my belly once more
To even entertain the thought
Of staying alive

These rough hands
Clutch artillery…
My creed is kill
Or be killed
Till death will my assailants bleed
Or shall I bleed

The fate
That lies before me
I know not
As I step over the decaying flesh
 Of war casualties
Because we were sent to die…
For another man's greed

NO TOILET PAPER

No toilet paper
Is
A no, no

Especially
When that moment comes
And there is no
Quilted fabric to wipe

Realization
Has never been so clear

Desperation
Has never been this near

And the
Classified ads
Have never
Felt so right

LAZYBONES

Another day
Has gone bye
And you have done nothing
But sat around
On yo lazy behind

You won't
Apply for a job
You excessively eat up food
You do not buy
And run up bills
You never help pay
And your nasty lifestyle
Has crossed the line

You never speak
Of successful achievements
And you fail to realize
That no one
Wants to take care
Of someone that's
Healthy and grown

Truth is
You've worn out
Your welcome
While exhausting
Our relationship
And it's time
You face responsibility
And take care of your own

BALLAD OF A BALD MAN

So dear
So precious
So close to the heart
Each hair follicle
Seems to be

One by one
They slowly fall
Like leaves in autumn
Stimulating insecurity

With hats and glasses
We disguise this flaw
Ashamed of letting it show

Looking for
Miracle breakthroughs
Of hair restoration
Hoping someday
That withering hair-do
Will finally grow

P.S. Women dig the clean baldheaded man
Not Bozo

HOMELESS IN JANUARY

How long
Can one bare temperatures
Below freezing

Without shelter
Heat
Food
Nor a bed for their
Heads to lie

Frostbitten
Bone agonizing winds
Torture the skin
Hyperthermia settles in

And if the lord
Cracks not the sky
To dry the frosting tears
That drip from withering eyes
Of lament…

Then the lament
Shall surely die

ENDANGERED SPECIES

The rise of robots
Is nigh

When man power
Is replaced by machines

Unemployment increases
And the crime rate
Is beyond your most wicked dreams

So if
All corporations
Invested in automation
Then how
Would the unemployed survive.

Without work
There's no income
No food
Nor shelter

So tell me

How will those people stay alive?

OLD FOLK YOUNG FOLK

Old folk have been blessed
With the gift of time and wisdom
But their shared knowledge
To the youth
Falls upon deaf ears
Because young folk
Sho knows it all

Many young folk
Have no respect for their elders
Who have paved the way
 For them to follow
So they don't have to fall

Old folk can see
The dark future that lies ahead
From footsteps of their past
But young folk laugh
And crack cowardly old jokes

But sad to say
That some young folk
Will never walk the path of the elders
While realizing on their death bed
How blessed it is to be
Old folk

OLD FOLK HAVE EXPERIENCED LIFE
AND HAVE GAINED WISDOM FROM IT
AND YOUNG FOLK DIE FROM THE LACK OF IT

IF I WERE BLIND

If I were blind
Could I perceive evil
Through the eye
Within my mind

Would darkness
Curse the universe
In which I dwell
Like a living hell
Till the end of time?

If I were blind
Would I be tempted
By the lust
That condemns the hearts of men?

If the blind
Had eyes
To witness the tribulation that awaits us
Would they long
To never see life again?

WAR AND GLORY

I Stare across
The battlefield of warriors
Who have the same ambitions as I
Driven by a flame
That burns within their time piece

For this one goal
You have to have passion
Dedication
Determination
Sweat burns my eyes
As I see the intensity
On this level increase

Many shall fall
For it is not their time
Others will stand their ground
And continue to strive

But out of the elite
Only one shall prevail
All the rest will kneel to the agony of defeat
Only the strong will survive

And I!
Am against all
Who stand before me
With a heart like fire

And a will of iron
As I stare into the eyes of Goliath
With no fear
In my quest to find glory

It is now time

FOR WAR!!

CORDS OF ELECTRIC

Rhythmic thunder
Played with fire and passion
When plectrum becomes intimate
With steel

Eyes tightly shut
As mind becomes one
With the body and soul
Of the instrument
Electrifying earlobes
Just man...and...instrument

Six strings scream
Tears of a strad
Sighing
The joys and pains
Of ones spirit and dreams
Like never before

Painting portraits
Of distant sunsets
Standing at the edge of ever
Racing against time
Until the last bead of sweat
Drips...

And kisses the floor
Then it's over

ONE YEAR DOWN AND TWENTY-NINE TO GO

For eight long hours
I walk up and down this line
Working my tired limbs to the bone

Along side hundreds of folks
With multiple problems
And disgruntled personalities
Stimulating fantasies
Of me resting
In the comfort of my own home

Supervisor
Continuously stressing me!
Pressing me!
This factory life
Is depressing me!

Father forgive me
For I have a confession--see
If one more person
Rubs me the wrong way
The authorities
Might be arresting me!

But once
My day is finally over

I'll wipe the sweat from my brow
Thinking how this strenuous day
Went by so slow

And I don't know
How much more I can take
With one year down
And twenty-nine more to go

Damn!

A CRY FOR UNITY

What's the purpose
Of having a union
If the union's officials
Lead their
Members astray?

Sadly
What was once
Considered
A solidified
Organization
Of brothers and sisters
Is none other
Than a weakened team
In disarray

If you
Deceive us
With your lies and secrets
We will
Forever stand divided

But
How can we possibly
Classify ourselves
As a union
If we never
Stand united?

DIVINE INSPIRATION

How many hearts
Can one touch

How many lives
Can one change

With words
That has an impact
On us all

Reaching
The souls of the masses

Restoring hope
Unto the less fortunate

Placing smiles
Upon the faces
Where tears of pain
Used to fall

OPRAH WINFREY

BALLAD FOR MY MOTHER

My dear
Sweet mother…
There's no word
Descriptive enough
To express the gratitude
That I feel for the things
That you have done for me

In time
You've persevered
The wilds I've put you through
And the reign of havoc
That life has reeked upon thee

As a youth
It was quite hard for me to see
All the struggles that you endured
And the sacrifices you had to make
Just to place
A roof over my head
The clothes on my back
A toy in my palm
And the precious meals
That you prepared for my plate

And over the years
You've never ceased to amaze me
With the uphill battles

That you've won
And never failed to raise me

As an adolescent
Getting out of line
You would get the belt
And blaze me

And the day
That I consider myself
Too grown to honor
The presence of my mother
Is the day that you color me crazy

Because you are
The mother
The friend
The doctor
The warden
The lawyer
The executioner
Love and strength
At its finest

And the moment
Somebody finds the nerve
To dispute me
About these words I speak
Is the day moment I declare
That fool blinded

Because you are…
The greatest

RESPOSIBILITIES

There's nothing precious
Quite like
Childhood memories

The joy of
Feeling free
And being able
To come and go
As you please

Enjoying every second
Of the day

Nightlife
City lights
And its cool breeze

But oh
How those good times
Seem to vanish
Like the evening sun
Into darkness
When we obtain
responsibilities

FAT MAN

All day he sits
And gluttony eats
Ice cream
Cakes
And pies

Damaging health
Love life
Moral
Self esteem
And a physique
That he will soon
Despise

LEAN ON ME

I can see
The scar of depression
Written all over your face
As you come to realize
How life's taste
Can make one
Long for their own demise

Sometimes
Life can be so relentless
Hostile
Acclimating ones mentality
To despair
No longer believing in
Still I rise

Yet this life
Is hard hitting

With a decline in economy
It allures one to engage
In a life that is forbidden

So I pray
That the lord
Illuminates the path
That leads us to
A brighter day

Then maybe
This troubling life
Won't seem to hurt so much

And that stress
That follows you diligently
Will cease to vex
Everything that you touch

So allow me
To be the wind beneath
Your wings
That will carry you
From this rut that binds you
Shackling your feet
To rock bottom
And I'll supply
Anything within my power
Plus a shoulder when you weep

So fear not
That your cries fall upon death ears
Because I hear you
And overstand that
You can lean on me

But where do I turn
When the flames of life burn

Beyond the point of my silence
My screams
So excruciating
Violent
That tears produce
From your eyes

Because I'm that reflection
In your pupil
With knees and knuckles
Embedded in mud

Due to struggle

Can you help me
I'll repay you two-fold
I give you my word
Written in blood

And all I ask
Is for that one who has my back
No matter what

So when I stare into
The eyes and beneath the skin
Of the one who carries me
I'll see the image of Jesus

IDLEWILD

Idlewild…

A place
Where my ancestors
Sought refuge
And some considered home

An oasis of peaceful spirits
So even in solitude
You're not alone

A land where
Legendary black musicians
And artist performed
Stimulating joy
And pleasant smiles

Oh how
Easy life feels
When strolling Daisy Street
In a place called Idlewild

There ain't a place in the world
Like Idlewild Michigan

PART TWO

Silent Screams

LUST AND DESIRE

TABOO

In an instant
She struck my world
Like a tempest
Multiplied by ten

Her physique
Was a rendition
Stimulating my thoughts of sin

And my infatuation
Seemed to be a condition
That I had not
The desire to alleviate
Although it had my head spinning

Like a fifth of gin
On a empty stomach
Leaving me longing for
Hydrogen and oxygen
Because she was hot like that

Plus baby girl was strapped
Stacked like MGM poker chips

Her sundress
Accentuated her voluptuous hips
That I longed to palm
To pull closer to remove every spec of gloss

From her lips with mine
Now that's taking it a little bit too far ain't it

Well that's just too bad
Because I must keep it real

I want to give her something
That she can feel

What would you do?
If she walked by you
Looking sexy and fine
As aged wine

Making you wanna
Finger stroke the feline
Till it showed signs that it was time

Then rewind her walk
Ninety-nine times
Jus to accumulate
Enough saliva in your mouth
To quench your thirst
Because I told you
That she was hot like that

But be alarmed
Those strong urges

Will have you blinded
With your nose wide open
And trippin' about things that ain't there
With heart pressed

And when you
Feel like you digging somebody
More than they're digging you
Emotions become dangerous

Evolving in your heart
Like a time bomb with four seconds left

As a kamikaze
Ready to detonate on anybody
That rubs you the wrong way
Because hurt feelings make you heartless

But anyhow
It's been a year now
Of our off and on
Flirtation and lusting

And she's having problems
I'm the one she confides and trust in
Before we lock eyes and lips
While inside we're combusting

I mean
It had got so deep
I could damn near
Feel myself inside of her
Without subtracting apparel

All while she's telling me
That I'm making her
Steamy and wet

Simultaneously
She's pecking my neck
And stroking my chest
Got me ready to blast off like NASA
Then softly she whispers
I can't give you none yet

Baby you know
That I'm feeling you
And games I'm not trying to play

But the only thing
That stands between you and me
Is the one I must introduce you to…
My fiancé

Sabrina!
Sabrina
Sabrina

SEXY SISTA

Gooooooodness!!!
Gracious!!!

Sexy sista
With thunda thighs
Bulging a brotha's eyes

You give me
Premonition

Of you
Me
Strawberries and melted chocolate
Spillin over your plump hills

In the heat
Of intense…
Coition

COFFEE BROWN

Ms Coffee Brown
Is unlike
Any other woman

Beauty
Intelligence
Soul
Sex appeal
Wrapped in an ebony shell
The epitome
Of an Ethiopian Queen

With eyes of fire
Hair natural
Smile shines like
Morning sunbeam

Hourglass figure
Marinated in caramel
Mahogany flesh
Looks sweet as
An orchid of nectarines

I mean
I aint never seen
A woman quite like you
Dwelling on this side of town

You are the finest thing around
To see you walk
Makes my heart pound
Ms Coffee Brown
Please answer me one question
My sista'

How…can I be…down?

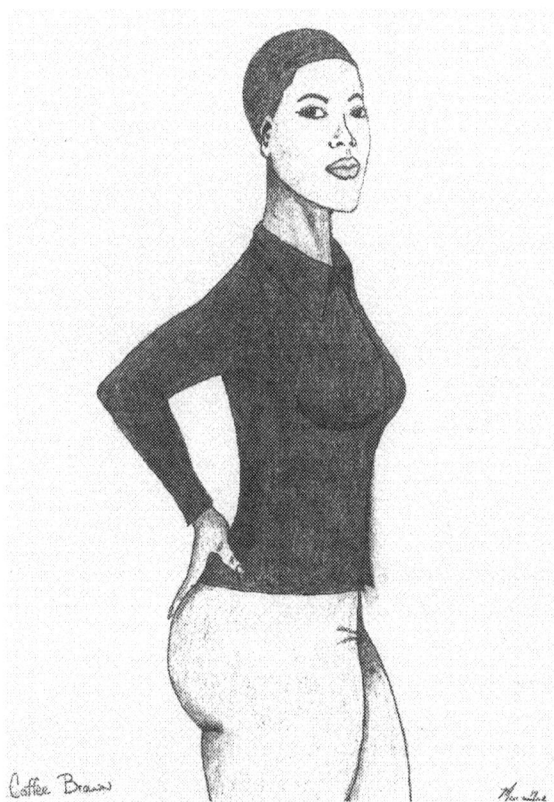

COFFEE BROWN

CHOCOLATE IN AN HOURGLASS

Through the windows
Of my soul appeared to me…
Chocolate in an hourglass

Her beautiful presence
Stunned me
I was momentarily speechless
For her I had tunnel vision
As my pulse began
Beating fast

Who was this woman
That I had never seen
True representation of a black queen
A goddess

And even though
She attracts eye contact
Beyond the laws of magnetism
Her personality was humble
And modest

I love that

Briefly
She drew my focus

And I explained everything
That I was thinking through my eye contact

I
Admired her
Feather wrap hair-do
As well as her molecular structure
From her shoulders
To the small of her back

Which led me
To the heart of her sexy walk
Every motion was so hypnotic

Please believe me

This woman
Mentally had me captivated
Stimulating fantasies
That are sensual
And erotic

Her outfit
Is exotic

Brotha
She gives her dress
A whole new definition

I was sippin'
My drink thinking
As we caught eye contact

She must have felt
My intuition

The vibe
Then changed positions
She said she had her eyes
On me all night
And didn't know what to say

Then she jotted her number
And said I hope to hear from you
Someday

And as she walked away
I blew a kiss
At a queen who possessed sex appeal
And class

As my eyes traced her every motion
Saying "Damn"
I just met chocolate in an hourglass

CHOCOLATE IN AN HOURGLASS

A SISTA'S PORTRAIT

Eye poppin'
Tongue soppin'
Make a fella say um, um, um
When he stares at this
Intriguing photo

Of flips
Feather wraps
And cornrows
Thick lips
Hips and voluptuous asses
In hourglass figures
Making brotha's thoughts pause
Like whoa!

Sexy
Erotic
Seductive
Hypnotic
Enticing
And captivating without a doubt

And there's
Nothing worth salivating for
More than a group of sista's
Posing
Staring back over their shoulders
With fingertips on hips
Slightly bent over
And juicy asses
Bulging out

A SISTA AND HER HAIR

Sistas
Love them some hair
And ya make damn sho
Ya lookin' fine

Some of 'em
Are well educated
And some of 'em
Dun lost they damn mind

Some can be
Jus' getting out the hair salon
And ain't got two nickels to rub together
Tryin' to find a way home
But one thang's for sho
She won't let the wind blow
Too hard on her hair-doo
And stay lookin' fine

Sista's keep numerous hair styles
One day she'll be Pocahontas
And the next day
She'll be as bald headed as Grace

Some sistas can barely walk
And chew bubble gum

But please believe
When its time for bed

She'll make damn sho she's sleepin' on her face

The scriptures say
That a woman's hair is her glory
Some of us don't overstand
How she can be glued to the mirror
Armed with brushes, combs and jam

But believe you me
It don't matter if she gets it from her momma
Or the beauty supply
She gone keep that wig done
How ever she can

FINGERTIPS AND TOES

There's nothing in the world
Quite like
A woman's sexy fingertips and toes

The phenomenal French manicure
Or
Sexy shades of red
Burgundy
Peach etc
Each color
Matching her beautiful selection
Of suits dresses and clothes

Her confidence shows
In every step takes
In every move she makes
And when men stare
At her gorgeous hands and feet

No matter what the complexion

French vanilla
Butter
Caramel
Chessnut
Mahogany
Russet
Cinnamon and chocolate

Silent Screams

They all look delicious and sweet

Making men
Long to kiss the concrete
That the soles of her feet have blessed

When I fantasize of her fingertips
I see my scalp
Being massaged
And caressed
By the hands of a goddess

Her fingernails
Look so seductive
By the way she holds her wine glass

Reflecting cleanliness
And class
Enticing when she
Clutches her breast and ass
Or when she
Straps those sexy looking feet
In those summer sandals
And walks pass

When a man holds
And kisses a woman's hands and feet
With passion

How long will she last
Before losing her clothes

Till dawn
It will show through intimacy
From a little attention and affection
To her sexy
Fingertips and toes

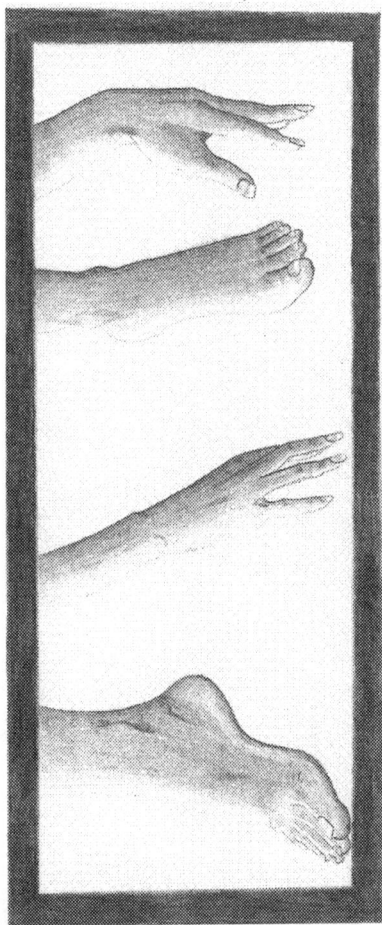

FINGERTIPS AND TOES

Silent Screams

PART THREE

Silent Screams

PASSION AND LOVE

ADORE

I love
The way that you look
The way that you walk
The way that you talk
The way that you smell

It is a delight
When the first thing
I recognize
In the morning
Is you
And the last thing
I remember seeing
Before I lay me down
To sleep

You are the reason
I smile when I dream

The shinning star
That brightens
My day

Truth is
I simply adore you

ENCHANTING

What is more romantic
Than a
Candle lit
Bubble bath

Serenaded by
Passionate melodies

Chocolate fondue and strawberries

Champagne for two

With you
And I
Enjoying the pleasure
Thereof...

Perhaps nothing

HOT TUB

Good lawd!
Baby you are
The epitome
Of jaw dropping sexy

Every curve
Of yo hourglass frame
I wish to explore

Allow my tongue
To catch the beads of water
That trickle from your flesh

And quench my thirst
With your
Forbidden fruit juice du jour

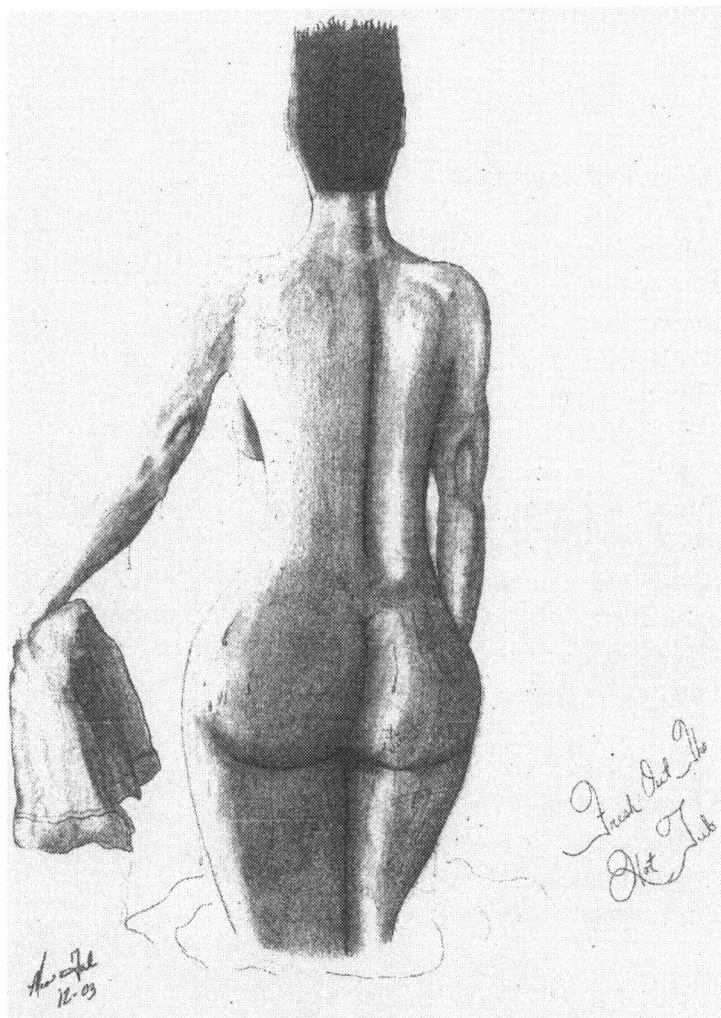

Fresh Out The
Hot Tub

HOT TUB

CLIMAX

Her eyes rolled upward
As their lids
Slowly closed
Parting toes
Embracing ecstasy
Soft kisses
Trace her earlobes

Easing down her neck
Swallowing sweet oils
Of tender breasts
Multiple faces manifest
Sporadic breaths
Moist tongue
Caresses her nipples

Affects ripple
Through her navel
Body quivers
Nectar conceives
From her forbidden fruit

Breathing increases
Parting thighs
Squinting eyes
Bed sheet rippin'
Head grippin'
Sweat drippin'
Passionate sighs

Vigorously
Nibbling, tasting, sucking
Tongue thrust
To her peach
Disabling speech
With each motion
Grinding teeth
Until tension
Peaked her climax

HER LIPS

Her lips
Full
Moist and thick

Passionately
Placed upon my lips
My chin
My neck
My chest

Stimulating
Erotic fantasies
And erection

Spellbinding

Soul trembles
With anticipation

Abdomen
Sensuously traced with her tongue
Southbound

Her hand
Clinching stiff flesh

I overzealously
Embrace her

Warm
Wet
Eye closing
Toe curling
Knee buckling
Breath taking
Back arching
Deep lunging kisses
Aggressively siphoning
Swallowing my nature
Like her life depended on it!

STRENGTH OF PUSSY

Pussy
Is the most
Sweet and deceptive thing
That you may ever encounter

There's nothing
Like the touch
Nor the taste
Nor the smell of pussy

And pussy knows this

Pussy knows
That you want it
Need it
Do any thing to gain it
Jeopardize your life to obtain it
Lord be with you if it's tainted
But pussy feels so damn good

How on earth can we resist it

But some of us
Don't overstand when pussy is restricted
Before you know it
They have touched
Sniffed
And licked it

Got addicted
And keep going to the well
Until the morons are convicted
For being involved with a minor
And that's some dumb shit

But on the other hand
Pussy will solidify
And make your day and night complete
From your crown to the concrete
You will feel like
The K.I.N.G of the H.E.A.P

Though some of us swear
That we're the P.I.M.P
Simultaneously
Pussy be fucking those same boys mentally
Leaving them blinded
And dependent upon her to see
That pussy will fortify your confidence
And eradicate it
Replacing it with insecurity

Pussy got some of you spellbound

Even got females lives turned upside down
Had on chic come cross town
Strapped with firearms and live rounds

To blow a brotha's house down

Because don't nobody taste her pussy but her

Plus pussy pays her bills
Buys her food and clothes

So if pussy got the fellas
Bringing in the doe
Can somebody please explain to me
Who's the playa and who's the hoe
Perhaps pussy might be the biggest pimp we know

But one things for sho
Pussy is a beautiful thing
Jus misused often

And I aint trying
To tell no one to deny pussy
But if you're smart you will approach it with caution

And never underestimate the strength of pussy

SPEND MY LIFE WITH YOU

Every moment
That we've shared
Has been
Nothing less
Than magical

Your spirit
Highlights my life
And to keep that light shinning
There's nothing
I wouldn't do

There's no greater feeling
Than to be loved dearly
By the one
You love so much

And if
God be willing
I pray
That I am blessed
To spend
The rest of my life
With you

LOVE'S WORTH

Everything
If it's true

SOUL MATE

Soul mate
I love you

I've dreamt of you
During my lonely cold nights

I've prayed
Wished
Waited
For the touch of your skin
And the easement of your voice
As I sit
Listening to the sound of rippling water
Under beams of moonlight

I close my eyes
Clutching wind
Fantasizing
Feeling your head upon my chest
As we rest till sunrise

And though
We're hundreds of miles apart
You're irreplaceable
In my heart
And I promise
I will love you
Till...
The end...
Of time

ONE

If there was ever one
Who touched my soul
And made my life complete

It would be you

The rose
Whose love has blossomed
In my heart
And has colored
My bitter moments sweet

So with this ring
I vow to love
And cherish thee always
As you bestow upon me
Light that shines
As bright as the morning sun

No longer
Are we two individuals
Yearning to fill
The void that was once between us
Because together
We equal
One

Silent Screams

PART FOUR

Silent Screams

WHEN RELATIONSHIPS CRUMBLE

OVERZEALOUS

Think not
That I despise you
Or have intensions
To treat you cold

But how can I
Possibly say
That I love you
If my mind
Is unfamiliar
With your soul

ISSUES

Why is it that
When you first
Meet someone…
They can be
So overzealous
And quick
To pursue
Relationships?

Why must I
Be considered
Full of games
Because my aim
Is not aligned
With
Obligation and commitment?

Why is it that
You feel
The right
And the nerve
To question
And check me
About my actions
That occurred
Within my personal time
If I am not yours
And you are not mine?

Why are you
So hypocritical
Claiming
That all of us
Are scum
When you're
The one
Chasing after the bad
But preaching
The good ones
Are hard to find?

YOU HAVE ISSUES!

PICTURE

From jump
I explained to you
That there was someone else
Presently in the picture

Yet you
Keep telling me
You can picture you and me
Holding hands in a picture
And placing it upon your mantel piece
I guess you refuse to get the picture

My endeavor
Is to sever myself
From a seven and a half year relationship
Filled to the brim
With tension and stress

My heart encased in a bulletproof vest
Excessive drama
Is too much to digest
Therefore anything more than friendship
Is prohibited from this picture
But how many times must I preach this
For this to hitcha

Besides
Bad break ups and rebounds

Are a bad mixture
Subject for backlash and retaliation

No time to recover
Premature lovers tend to build new homes
On old foundations
Wanting not to embrace this tribulation

So please
Allow me room to rejuvenate
And breathe
No need to be rushie

Love by pressure
Not by will
Can get real ugly
Trust me

Must we switch gears
And pretend you never listened
In the beginning of our conversation

That we were to be
Stress-less lover friends
Without damaging feelings
With no chance for reconciliation

This whole ordeal has become annoying
Those cellular conversations are now draining

Dividing my personal time
Becomes mandatory
As patience evaporates due to complaining

And I despise feeling compelled
To have to explain
My day to you in detail

Too much pressure makes one claustrophobic
Yearning for space and solitude to exhale

Sexual intercourse derails
A perfect invitation for cheating and pain

Verbal abuse and bad names
Surface due to the fact
That you're trying to force
Something that ain't ready to happen
And can't be maintained

Baby slow ya roll and take it easy
Before you destroy a beautiful thing…
Get the picture

WHEN RELATIONSHIPS CRUMBLE

When relationships crumble
Tears fall
And faces frown

Hearts get torn
While pondering
How love turned upside down

Anger grows
As memories surface
Someone has to be
Charged for pain

Heartless actions
Are hard to forgive
I guess
I'll never
Fall in love again

CAN'T LET IT GO

Some say
The second time around
Is the sweetest

The loving
Is greater
After the wounds are healed
And there's
Nothing left to do
But grow

And despite
The scars of betrayal we've faced
And the pain that we've endured

We refuse find it
Reason enough
To let what we have
Go

GONE

Take not for granted
The love that I offer you
Because it will not
Always be

For the moment
Will come
When you shall
Reach out for me

And I'll be
Long gone
Leaving you with nothing
But a memory

APOLOGY

For the first time
I know what true love is
Yet my grasp for it
Appears to be too late

You gave me
Your heart and soul
Unconditionally
But the fruit you bestowed upon me
I did not appreciate

Countless times
Have you turned the other cheek
Condoning my wrongs
And I never took the time
To overstand it

Tomorrow never promises
The warmth of a pure heart
And I realize that
True love
Is not to be taken for granted

My call for your name
Seems to fall upon deaf ears
And for once
Pain and pity
Fills my lamenting eyes

Which bare tears
Of a lonely soul
With only prayers and hope
That you will see
That I sincerely…

Apologize

BEFORE WE SLEEP

Before we sleep
Let us make peace
And put an end
To the bitterness thereof

Let us kiss
Before we sleep
And wake up
Sharing utopian dreams
That reflect the fruits
Of our love

Let us forgive
Before we lay
That yesterday's problems
Curse us not today

The family
That prays together
Stays together
And if that be so
Then let us pray

WHY

Love is not
Malicious words
Making someone cry

Love is not a
Raging fist
Blackening one's eye

Love is not
Life threatening incidences
That made
Thousands like you die

So why
Do you choose
Not to leave a situation
That is detrimental
To the precious life
That you were given…

Why?

SEPARATE WAYS

Perhaps
We never knew
Each other
Like we thought
We did

Beyond sexual intercourse
We were nothing more
Than strangers
Trying to coexist

Neither
Time or friendship
Was considered

Heartache and tears
Seem to be
The only thing
We have in common

Therefore
It be better
To live happily alone
Than to be with someone
Killing me softly

PART FIVE

Silent Screams

ONCE IT'S OVER

NO MORE US

What was thought
To be a match made in heaven
Is now just a vague image
Of bitter memories

A love once appended
In the depth of my heart
Like the roots of an oak tree
Was violently hewn down
By the cold blade
Of misery

Two hearts
Torn apart by lust
Suffering a great deal of pain
That was unjust

In my solitude
I sit with
Candle and portrait of us
Watching as frozen time
Slowly combusts

TRAP

Relationships
Are dangerous
When a woman
Is motivated by greed

Loving someone
For their soul
Is jus a facade
That she portrays
When inside
She is driven
By his prominence
And financial stability

But once
Her dreams appear to fade
And a promising future
Is hard to see

The art
Of seduction
And the pleasure love making
Will be her most
Fascinating weapon
She will use it
To trap him
With his seed

BABY MAMMA DRAMA

Woman!
You remind me
Of Emily Rose
From the Exorcist

Nine-eleven
Sodom hue sane
Satan and Hades
All wrapped up into one

A curse
Or a plague vexing my soul
With words
That are cold as snow in Moscow
Can somebody
Please tell me how…
Many cups of gin
How many fifths of Hennessey
And how many kegs of rum

Did I drink
That day that I met you
When I let you
Into my life
And rearrange it
To the point I longed
To stop breathing

Receiving oxygen
A friend you never were
I must concur with the rest
And confess that you
Are filled with demons

Heathen
Some of yall
Should've been swallowed semen

Cause hellions like you
 Keeps me screaming!

MO' DRAMA

Gooooood lawd!!!!

Why did I
Foolishly plant my seed
In the womb
Of the devil's child

Spellbound was I
By the voluptuous curves
Of her flesh
Simultaneously blinded
By the gleam
Of her
Deceptive smile

How on earth
Did I French kiss
The lips of a snake
For so long
Without being alarmed
By the rattling
Of her tail

Her miserable soul
Longs the weeping of my eyes
And the wail
Of my lamenting cries
As she continuously tries
To acclimate my life
To the tribulation
Of her living hell

YOUNG MOTHER

She was young
Hot
And sizzling
Couldn't keep her legs closed
Giving birth
At age thirteen

Poor excuse for a role model to her child
Who learned by example
And did the same as she

Hard times
Had just gotten harder
She needed lots of money
So she hustled
And turned tricks

And never
Really enjoyed
Sweet life as a youth
Once she became a grandmother
At twenty-six

A HOE

A hoe is
As a hoe does

Utilizing sex
For monetary gain
Is her story

Whether it be
At the motel
In the back seat of a car
Or casually in the comfort
Of her own home
And it doesn't matter
If it's with
Someone she knows

Her classification
Is self-explanatory

She's
A hoe

MICHIGAN AVE.

Corner of Michigan Ave.
And Livernois
Funky asses hustle to their
Favorite spot
When night falls
Hoping for a bit of luck

Sleazy
Short
Tight
Provocative dresses
Seductively
Showing thighs
Making one's nature rise
Offering a good suck
For a fast buck

All night you will see
Cars pull on and off
The strip
Where fellas are willing
To go broke for a piece of ass
And a quick blast

All night
Men pull in and out
In and out
The lips and asses
Of filthy hoes
That trick upon Michigan Ave.

BALLAD OF A FATHERLESS CHILD

Father

Father

How do you live your life
As if I do not exist

I
Your spitting image
Left with no other choice
But to face this merciless world
Without guidance
Is gravely unfortunate

How can a lost child
Survive the wilds of a cold world
Without remorse nor compassion
For the child
That is unlearned

You can abandon me
But there will be
No escape from the haunting whispers
Of skeletons
That lurk within the shadows
Of your mind
That will curse you
Till the day your ashes
Are completely burned

Silent Screams

PART SIX

Silent Screams

SILENT SCREAMS

Silent Screams

DIARY OF A SLAVE

Why is it I
That must cry these tears
Of severe pain and stress

I hang here
Tied by my blistered hands
The sun torches my skin
Sweat burns my wounds
As blood drips the rips of my flesh

With no remorse they still beat me
Because I was too weak to carry on
In these fields of cotton

This torment that I feel
Will be felt through future generations
And though my tears may dry
This pain will never be forgotten

Dear holy
And everlasting God
My father I come to you
Inside my prayers

With sorrows
Wishes and hopes
And though your voice
Beats not my eardrums

Your presence is felt
I know you're there

Please stop this torture lord!

With a two inch blade
They cut me down
My knees buckle on impact
My head bangs the hard dry gravel
As I see pieces of my bloody flesh
As food for insects on this cursed grounds

I wish dear lord
That could just obtain my own land
Create my own rules for myself
And be my own man

I am
The blood that drips down
Those tired black hands
That pick cotton from there fields

I am the soul
Of many who were sold
On cheap side street
Who were afflicted and almost killed

I am he with the tree on his back
Scared for life
From relentless blows
From their treacherous whips

I am he
Who stared into his fathers eyes
Who was beaten to his last breath
As blood seeped from his lips

I wish that I could vote
And have some say so
On who commands the land on which I stand

Or the freedom to speak
As I please
Without being broken to my knees
Or shot in the back of the head like my brother
In his quest for freedom as he ran

I wish
I wish
I wish oh Lord
I wish that I could
Just be me

I fantasize
Of breaking these chains
And flying away
Just as the Raven
I wish
That I could just be free

TREE OF WELTS

Silent Screams

BROTHA MAN

From the cradle
To the grave
The brotha man
Will always be
Considered a target

Young product of the block
Vexed with adversity
Has no other choice
But to endure
What life has in store
No matter how hard
It gets

So in his quest
To find success
He chases rap careers
And hoop dreams
As a means
To make ends touch

And though
He faces
The unthinkable
And has to overcome
The impossible
It is a must
That brotha man
Never gives up

CAPTIVE

From the slave ships
To the cotton fields
The Blackman
Was chained

From the cotton fields
To the auction blocks
The Blackman
Was chained

And although
Slavery was abolished
His freedom
Is still restrained

Due to
A series
Of the most
Unfortunate circumstances
That has the Blackman
Still chained

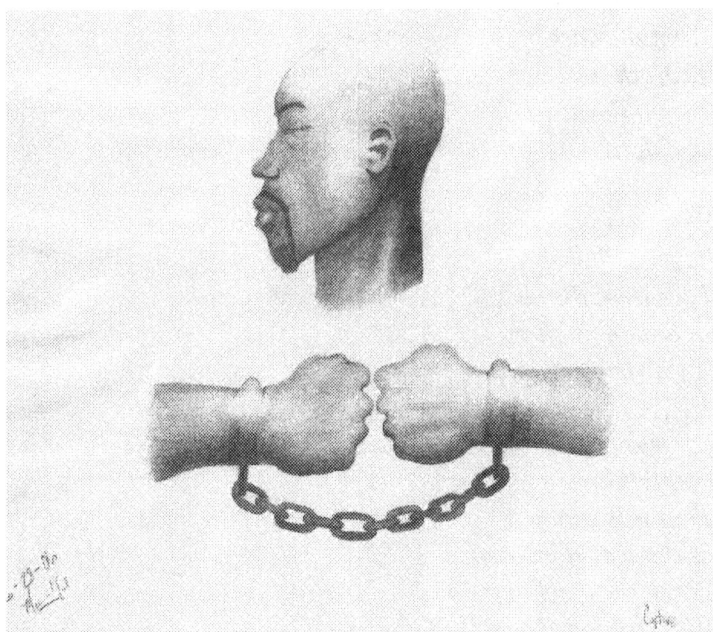

CAPTIVE

VIGILANTE

Die!
His black shottie screamed
From the dark
As death
Ceased the heart
Of a devil

For every
Layer of flesh
Torn from the backs
Of beaten mothers
With vicious whips

For every
Father's neck
That was snapped
In the eyes of his seed
When the lynching
Was concluded…

Long live the soul
Of the vigilante

Nat Turner

The rebel

APPETITE FOR WAR

How old
Must one be
Before one realizes
That serenity
Should be
Sought after
Before violence

How many
Lives must
Be destroyed
And families
To mourn and suffer
Before the screams
Of self-destruction
Are brought
To silence

How much
Fire has to burn
And how much
Smoke shall rise
From the ashes
After the voice
Of disaster roars

How many
Souls must be lost
And pints of blood
Will saturate
The earth

Before we lose
Our appetites
For war?

DEATH OR A CELL BLOCK

If all we know
Is what we're taught
What we see
And what we hear
Going on around us
Then tell me
What is it
That you expect of me

At ten years old
I was told
I had to be the man
Of the household

I see mamma struggling
Utilities are on illegally
We barely making ends meet
You do the math!
We're broke...
So therefore a college degree
For me is just a fantasy

A fantasy
I need to become reality
To endure these hard times
In life
Which burden my soul

Slowly my mind
Becomes acclimated to strife

Premeditated departure
With razorblade
Pondering blood seeping wrist

Hardly has my tongue
Tasted life's bliss
Hell becomes fist
Reigning upon my mind
Not much longer can I
Endure this bullshit!

This bullshit
Of being a have-not

And over time
My efforts of trying to find
Legitimate employment have declined
Because minimum wage
Does not supply
Me with enough funds
For me to feed my family
Pay my rent
And get by

So I plot

I turn to the streets
And purchase a pound
Of cocaine
And a seventeen shot Glock
Soon
Many like me follow
Coffins are no longer hollow
Quickly they become filled
As teddy bears
And cards hang
On trees and phone poles
In memory of those
Who once
Roamed my block

Lord be with me
As I walk
Through the valley
Of the shadow of death
Because he
Who rides upon the pale horse
Follows me

With bloody shoes
Upon my feet
I walk hand in hand
With Shaytaan
As he leads me

Through paths of adversity
And I'm lost

Lost within the confines
Of a surreal state of mind

Which is intoxicated
To momentarily escape
These hard times
Wishing
I could rewind time
To redefine my past

The two dearest friends
No longer stand
Because
Just before my eyes
They faced their demise
After falling
Due to a fatal gun blast

And me!
I'm the young black male

A product of the system

Running from a broken home!
Running from narcotics!

Running from cops!
Running from gun shots!
Running from grave lots!

This is my life
My life
My life
My life

Got a brotha
Running
Running
Running
Running
Running for my life
I'm facing death or a cellblock

GANGSTA'Z FATE

A gangsta is
As a gangsta does

Follows
The rules established
And remains
Heartless

But even
Some of the most
Infamous gangstaz
Are unable
To escape the wrath
Of being institutionalized

Nor
Elude the kiss…
Of violent death

NUMBERED STEPS

Every man's foot steps
Are questioned

What is the unseen number
Placed upon the souls of a man's feet

Is there a way
For man to have footsteps eternally
That his flesh decay not
Beneath the concrete

Every step that was taken
Is just a memory
There are not eyes
To see how many footsteps
There are to come

No feet are promised
To bare the heat
Of tomorrow morning's sun
So let us
Step in wisdom and thanks
Because one day there could be none

COUNT EVERY STEP THAT IS TAKEN
AS A BLESSING

DEATH

Death
Is a miserable phantom
Who comes silently
To find her mate

Passing bye many
Stroking the brow of some
With her fingertips
But it's whom she French kisses
That suffers her fate

From the newborns
To the old and hunched
No one can see this specter
As she passes through

In the presence of family
Or in the depth of your sleep
Perhaps she wants to be
Intimate with you

STAY IN PRAYER

DEATH

SPILLED LIQUOR

Torn hearts
Tear drops
Hugs are given
As peers commemorate the soul
Of a dear friend

Joyful smiles
Manifest while
Staring at portraits
Of frozen time
Prior to life's tragic end

After one's ghost
Transcends this flesh shell
This living hell
And their last gasp for breath
Is complete

Cups tilt
Spilling Hennessey
Onto the concrete
In memory

Until we meet again
Rest in peace Homie

BALLAD FOR AN ANGEL

The gift
Of walking with you
In the flesh
And sharing with you
My life and times
Was as precious
As a diamond

Like a country sunrise
Your wonderful smile
Would illuminate
The day

There are
So many
Joyful memories
Of you
That I will cherish
For as long
As I have a pulse

Enabling me to smile
Knowing that
We will embrace each other again
In the afterlife
Someday

CEASE FIRE

Tear drops
And blood
Still stain
The concrete
Where my brothers
Heart took
Its last beat

Chalk outlines
Black corpses
And shell cases
As sorrow scars
Our mother's faces

One too many
Funerals
Our families attend
As we watch
Our youth
Being carried
By their
Best of friends

So we pray
Waiting on the day
To transpire
That our ghetto youth
Will realize
It is a must
That we cease fire

Silent Screams

PART SEVEN

Silent Screams

THE REVOLUTION

WHAT HAPPENS

What happens
When the black child
Is no longer deprived
The complete truth
About their history

What happens
When that child
Is convinced
Not to magnify
Black history month
But black history period

What happens
When that child
Selects
The great
Black leaders of old
As hero's
Such as
Medgar Evers
Huey Newton
Sojourner Truth
And
Malcolm X...
And they follow

What happens
When that child's
Sole ambition
Is to
Expose the system
That flourishes
From their misfortunes…
And they overcome

What happens
When the unconscious
Become alarmed

What happens
When the listeners
Believe

What happens
When more leaders
Are inspired

What happens…
When their words
Contain the impact
Of a grenade
Shattering
The dark glass
Of genocide

And black men realize
That they
Are not enemies
But allies
Configuring an army
From Detroit
To Long Beach
To the Five Boroughs
Etc.

What happens
When that child
Takes his history personally
Personifying
The life
Of the leaders
That came
Before him
And it becomes
An honor
And a privilege
To be black

What happens

When I spark
The revolution

THE VISION

I am
The voice of the unheard
The have-nots
Urban life

See my face
In the tears
That trickle down my sister's face
For having to face
Raising three children
On minimum wage
By her damn self

So don't cry sista'
Stay strong, and keep moving
The sun will shine

Just as the wolf
I stand in the depth
Of the wild
And in the moon light I
Raise my head and call
Howling for all
Young black males

From everywhere
Black feet
Come swiftly

I am the force
That drives them
As they run in packs

Am the breath
That they can't catch
And the heartbeat
As it skips track

I embrace the impact
Of their passion and pain
And release the scream
Of five-million Nubian kings
Inducing thunder and rain
While cracking the Red Sea
So that I can lead
Our future leaders
To psychological freedom

This is my vision
As the Voice

LITERARY LEADERS

Literary leaders

From your mouth
Spill hidden secrets
Of the world
As you awakening
The sleep

Leading the blind
To an oasis of prosperity
With gifted tongues
Illuminating the
Dark paths
Of the lost sheep

Multitudes
Are uplifted
Due to the
Strength of word
As far as the mind
Can see

Your lyrics
Pierce the psyche
Like the apex of the Kitana
As our souls embrace
The mastery of poetry

DEDICATED TO
ABIODUN OYEWOLE
UMAR BIN HASSAN
BABATUNDE
THE LAST POETS

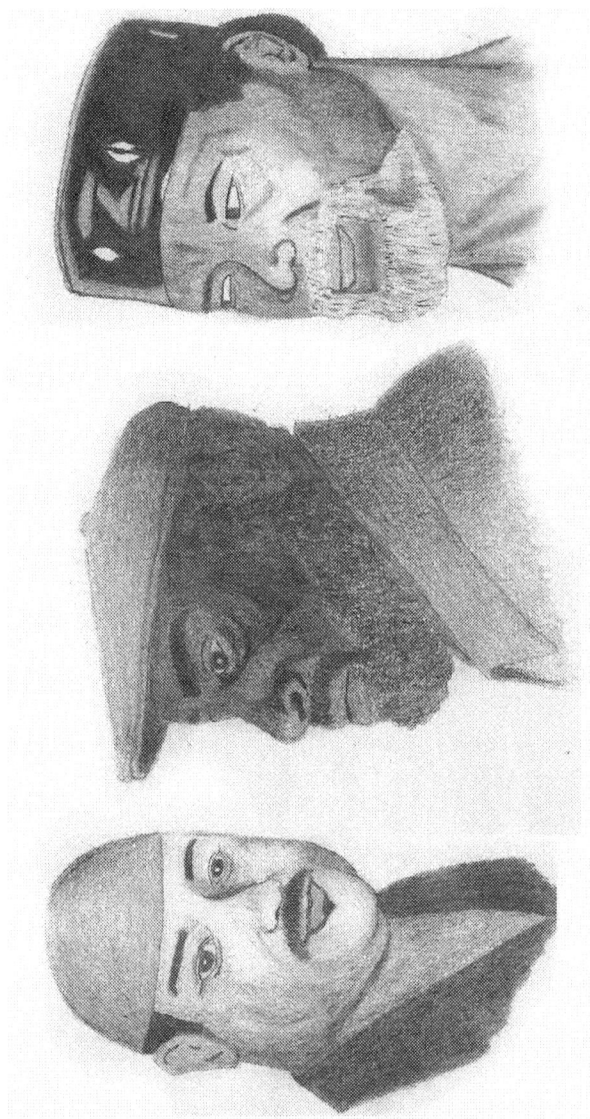

THE LAST POETS

BLACK UNITY

Today is the day
That the Blackman
Shall love
His fellow black brother
And no longer
Destroy his black brother

Today is the day
That we shall
Honor our
Beautiful black sisters
As queens
And by all means
Respect our mothers

Today is the day
That I will at least
Spend a dollar
With a black business
And help strengthen
Our community

To day is the day
I no longer stand against
My black brother
But with
My black brother
And show the world
The strength
Of black unity

IF MY WORDS HAD NO PURPOSE

Words represent
Life
Love
Hate
Passion
Pain
Peace
War
Us!

Words contain the strength
To uplift a decaying nation

From humiliation
To being doctors and teachers
M.L.K. had a dream
Of black and white unity
And from his dreams
To the manifestation of his words
He still lives
Even through the event of his assassination

My words make some long for my silence
For the exposal of truth being my endeavor

Perhaps I will see sunsets
For four score and ten years
But via my words
I shall dwell amongst you as a ghost
After my demise for ever

My ambition
Is to reach the minds of the people
That they may
Hold their heads high
And raise the fist

For love
Pride
And solidarity under god
But if my words had not a purpose…
Then I would not exist

Silent Screams

ABOUT THE AUTHOR

It all began December 19th, 1973 on Detroit's Westside. Melvin and Evelynn Christian gave birth to a son who would someday have an impact on people with the strength of words, and would be known by the name of
Men-Tal.

Like many black ghetto youths, Men-Tal's life was far from the so-called American dream, living it up in a plush home with a white picket fence, and a dog in the yard. It was more like a declining neighborhood infested with crack houses, dope fiends, graffiti scarred liquor stores, and abandoned buildings destroyed by the sixties riots. At night you could hear the sounds of gunfire echoing from house to house soon followed by the wail of police and ambulance sirens.

Those hard times make us appreciate' and cherish the few moments of happiness, and peace we find throughout the day to day troubles we face. When you can look out your window, and see beautiful children having fun playing four square, double-dutch, it's sort of like watching sun rays pierce through the dark clouds of a violent storm that has calmed. These same images would passionately be reflected upon through Men-Tal's words as he gives a descriptive view of what life is like through his eyes, and perhaps make a beautiful difference in someone's life. What do you expect from one who is the product of such an environment?

Men-Tal is the author of multiple books of poetry and novels accompanied by his detailed illustrations. *Silent Screams* is the first book released.

Men-Tal exhibits his work by performing at various venues in Detroit Michigan, and other cities, and states as well.

LOOK FOR UPCOMING ADDITIONAL WORKS BY POET AND ARTIST MEN-TAL

Please contact the poet/artist regarding:
- ❖ *Upcoming book signings*
- ❖ *Additional book purchases*
- ❖ *Original artwork*
- ❖ *Other projects by the poet/artist*
- ❖ *Other inquiries*

He can be reached by email at:

vegaz_313@yahoo.com